D0487975

FIFTY
BICYCLES
THAT
CHANGED
THE
WORLD

**DESIGN
MUSEUM**

FIFTY
BICYCLES
THAT
CHANGED
THE
WORLD

**ALEX
NEWSON**

FIFTY
BICYCLES

FIFTY
BICYCLES

The bicycle is the most popular form of transport ever created. Because of its popularity and ubiquity, the bicycle is a machine we are all familiar with. As an archetype, the bicycle has been established since the creation of the safety bicycle in the late nineteenth century. Like other successful archetypes, such as the four-legged chair, money and the telephone, the basic form of the bicycle has remained largely unchanged.

In essence, bicycles are simple machines, designed to take energy generated by the body's most powerful levers – the legs – and transfer it to the wheels. The mechanism that bicycles use to do this is a transparent one. The human eye can read this mechanism intuitively, appreciating how power is transferred from the legs to the wheels via the cranks and chain. Even the more complex elements such as the gears and brakes rely on simple mechanical solutions. In our increasingly digital world the bicycle remains unashamedly analogue.

Not all bicycles are the same, however. High-end performance bicycles are uniquely specialized, allowing athletes to excel at a particular discipline, while city run-arounds need to provide comfort, storage potential and longevity, and all within a particular price bracket. Essentially, the bicycle represents different things to different people, be it personal transportation, freight, a hobby, sport, exercise and very often a passion.

The Columbia safety bicycle, first produced by the Pope Manufacturing Company.

LAUFMASCHINE

c.1817
Baron Karl von Drais

While human-powered two-wheeled vehicles have been around in various guises for hundreds of years, it wasn't until the arrival of the Laufmaschine in 1817 that they first became a viable and relatively widely used form of transport. The Laufmaschine – which literally translates as 'running machine' – was conceived by the German civil servant Baron Karl von Drais (1785–1851) as an alternative method of transportation to the horse so that he could navigate the narrow tracks of the forestry estate where he worked.

Following on from previous two-wheeled vehicles, the Laufmaschine used in-line wheels and was constructed predominantly from wood. However, the addition of a rudimentary steering mechanism set the Laufmaschine apart from previous designs. As well as providing the rider with the obvious benefit of directional control, steering also had a dramatic effect on balance. The ability to make small adjustments to the front wheel enabled the rider to rebalance their weight and stay seated on the Laufmaschine without the need to touch the floor. This remarkably automatic reaction is something that we all acquire, through instinct as much as anything else, when we first learn how to ride a bike.

The Laufmaschine proved extremely popular and similar designs, known by various names including dandy horses and hobbyhorses, were soon being manufactured by enthusiasts and coach builders all over the world.

Karl von Drais saw the Laufmaschine as having potential to be sold across Europe. These Illustrations are taken from a prospectus von Drais sent to the Prince of Fürstenberg in 1817 in an attempt to raise financial backing for the machine.

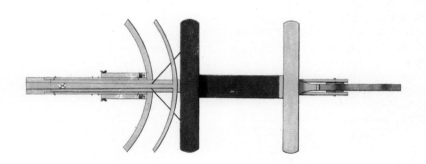

DIE *LAUFMASCHINE* DES
Freiherrn Carl von Drais.

VELOCIPEDE

c.1863
Pierre Michaux /
Pierre Lallement

The next major step in the evolution of the bicycle came with the introduction of mechanical propulsion. Prior to this, bicycles were usually pushed along by the rider's feet using a motion similar to running. There is some dispute as to who was responsible for first introducing pedals, with two different Parisian metalworkers both having valid claims on the invention. Around 1863 both Pierre Michaux (1813–83) and Pierre Lallement (1843–91) began manufacturing designs with rotary cranks and foot pedals attached to the front wheel hub.

Other experiments in mechanical propulsion included foot-operated treadles, which were similar to the foot panels used to drive looms and sewing machines. However, these solutions were never particularly practical and it wasn't until the late 1860s that bicycles using pedals similar to ones we recognize today were in widespread use. These came to be known as velocipedes – from the Latin for 'fast foot'.

While these designs did allow far greater speeds to be achieved, they were not without their problems. Pedals attached to the front hub made it very difficult to steer and pedal simultaneously and the poor ride quality gave rise to the nickname 'bone shaker'. As the velocipedes improved, and cyclists became more aware of their capabilities, cycling clubs started to form and the first organized races were held.

A typical image of a cyclist on a velocipede or 'bone shaker' bicycle, widely used throughout the 1840s and 1850s. This type of bicycle earned its moniker through the use of solid wood or metal wheels.

HIGH WHEELER /
PENNY-FARTHING

The penny-farthing, or high wheeler as it was more commonly known, evolved from the velocipede as engineers and manufacturers realized that the larger the wheel the farther one would travel with a single rotation of the pedals. These designs coincided with advances in metalworking that enabled stronger, lighter and more complex frames to be constructed.

As the popularity of high wheelers increased, manufacturers started to deliver an ever-increasing range of models. Each new model provided small improvements in areas such as handling, spoke and wheel tension, and advances in drivetrain mechanics. Riders could also choose a machine that best corresponded to the length of their leg.

Regardless of these advances, some fundamental problems remained. Mounting and dismounting a high wheeler was notoriously difficult as the saddle could be well over a metre (3ft 3in) high and the vehicle needed to be in motion before the rider could take a seat. They were also incredibly dangerous machines that needed skill and, more importantly, courage to ride. It was the frequent incidents and crashes involving high wheelers that gave rise to the phrase 'taking a header'.

A postman delivers mail using a penny-farthing. The speed and efficiency that the bicycle may have introduced to the postal service was undoubtedly countered by the number of accidents!

SAFETY BICYCLE

c.1880
Henry J Lawson

The earliest example of a rear wheel chain-driven bicycle is a drawing that appears in Leonardo da Vinci's *Codex Atlanticus* of c.1493. A design by the British inventor Henry J Lawson (1852–1925) of 1879 was in all probability the first chain-driven bicycle of real significance.Chain drives enabled a large sprocket attached to the pedal cranks to be connected to a small sprocket attached to the rear wheel. This simple mechanism multiplied the ratio of pedal revolutions to wheel revolutions, thus eliminating the need for the large wheels featured on high wheelers and precipitating a return to bicycles with smaller, similarly sized wheels.

The basic drive-chain system was further improved by John Kemp Starley (1854–1901), often described as the father of the bicycle industry, when he created the Rover Safety in 1885. The safety bicycle, as it became known, helped cycling become an accessible method of transportation and recreation, regardless of the cyclist's size, sex or fearlessness. As a journalist for *The Cyclist* commented upon seeing one of these bicycles for the first time: 'Here indeed is safety guaranteed, the cyclist may ride rough-shod over hedges, ditches and other obstacles without the fear of going over the handles'.

With this single innovation the modern bicycle was born. Almost every bicycle designed since has used mechanical and engineering principles derived from the safety bicycle.

There were many variations of the safety bicycle, with different manufacturers putting their own individual spin on the design. However, advertisements like this one from 1888 helped the Rover Safety bicycle become the most successful version of the era.

STARLEY & SUTTON,

Meteor Works, West Orchard,

COVENTRY.

"The 'Rover' has set the fashion to the world."—*Cyclist.*

18½ MILES IN THE HOUR; **30½** MILES IN **1** hr. **41** min. ON THE HIGH ROAD.

The "Rover," as ridden by Lord BURY, President N.C.U.

MANUFACTURERS OF THE CELEBRATED

"ROVER" BICYCLE,

THE "ROAMER" & OTHER TRICYCLES,

"COVENTRY CHAIR," &c., &c.

Price Lists and Testimonials Free.   Full Illustrated Catalogue, 2 Stamps.

SHAFT-DRIVEN BICYCLE

c.1890
Walter Stillman

Today we are accustomed to seeing a chain and the corresponding drivetrain as part of a bicycle. Chains and sprockets are exposed on the overwhelming majority of bicycles and are part of what we recognize in the form and shape of a bicycle. However, chain drives are not the only means of transferring power to the wheels.

The shaft drive is the most popular alternative drivetrain. The shaft-drive mechanism is typically comprised of a stiff rod, or drive shaft, with a bevelled gear at each end positioned at 90 degrees to the shaft. First patented in the United States by Walter Stillman in 1891, they initially proved popular. However, their use declined as chain-driven bicycles offered greater efficiency and the ability to work with a wider range of gearing systems, including derailleurs.

While the shaft drive's relative inefficiency makes the system unsuitable for racing or any form of elite performance, there has been a resurgence in manufacturers using them for urban bikes designed for frequent, short cycles. This is predominantly because the drive system can be built as an enclosed and sealed component, eliminating the need for regular maintenance and protecting the rider from the oil and lubrication required for a chain-drive design.

This early example of a shaft-drive design is a Columbia safety bicycle and was produced by the Pope Manufacturing Company in 1899. There are numerous examples of shaft-drive in current production; notable examples include Ross Lovegrove's Bamboo bike for Biomega.

DURSLEY PEDERSEN BICYCLE

1894
Mikael Pedersen

The Pedersen bicycle is one of history's more idiosyncratic and unusual-looking designs. The machine's designer, Mikael Pedersen (1855–1929), was a Danish blacksmith, inventor, musician and keen cyclist. Pedersen was responsible for an eclectic range of machinery, including a threshing machine that separated the wheat from the chaff, a gearing system for horse-driven mills, a braking system for carriages, and a centrifuge for separating cream that helped to revolutionize the dairy industry.

In 1893 Pedersen moved from his native Denmark to Dursley, England and applied for a patent for a new type of bicycle. He was unhappy with the comfort afforded by the orthodox safety bicycles of the time, claiming that they were 'weakest where they ought to be strongest and heaviest where they ought to be lightest'. To rectify this, Pedersen set about reconfiguring the entire machine, starting with the element he found most troubling – the saddle.

Pedersen's design for a new flexible saddle resembled a woven sling that worked according to the same principles as a hammock. A frame constructed from 14 narrow steel rods was then designed around the saddle. Based on solid engineering principles, the complex geometry of the resulting bicycle consists of 21 distinct triangles and 57 separate joints.

Although the Pedersen bicycle was first produced in the 1890s, the unique look and ride quality of the original design have ensured that it continues to be built today, albeit in relatively small numbers.

TRADITIONAL DUTCH *OMAFIETS*, OR 'GRANDMA'S BIKE'

The traditional Dutch bicycle, or *omafiets* – meaning 'Grandma's bike' in Dutch – evolved following the introduction of the safety bicycle and the rapid industrialization of bicycle production in the Netherlands at the end of the nineteenth century. First designed in 1892 by Royal Dutch Gazelle, the Netherlands' largest cycling brand, the *omafiets* is still in production and remains largely unchanged today.

The predominantly flat Dutch landscape is perfect for leisurely cruising around on a bicycle, and, like any successful product, the *omafiets* is entirely suited to its environment. The rear luggage rack is strong enough to take the weight of a person and the lowered step-through crossbar available on some models helped women use the *omafiets* while wearing skirts or dresses. The gently hooped frame, metal chain-guard, curved handlebars and extreme upright riding position result in an instantly recognizable machine.

Built from steel, almost uniformly finished in black, the *omafiets*' solid and rugged construction ensured that they were built to last a lifetime. As common today as any point over the past hundred years, many owners are, quite literally, riding their grandma's bicycle.

Dutch Gazelle were awarded their 'Royal' epithet by Princess Margriet in 1992. The Dutch Royal Seal of approval is granted only to successful Dutch brands that have existed for more than one hundred years and are exceptionally influential in their field. Since the company's foundation in 1892 in excess of 12 million Gazelles have been produced.

THE TANDEM

It is almost impossible to pinpoint the exact origins of the tandem. While bicycles designed for more than one person, in various incarnations, have been around since the mid nineteenth century, one of the first documented examples was a two-seater built by Mikael Pederson (see page 18) in 1898.

Tandem riding provides a completely unique and rewarding experience, one that differs significantly from the experience of a single-seater. In allowing two people, of differing strength, endurance and ability, to ride together, the tandem can turn an individual activity into a shared experience. This fact helped tandem riding initially gain popularity as a romantic pastime indulged in by lovers. Tandem riding is now more widespread, with other common uses including providing access to cycling for people with a range of physical and visual impairments.

Riding a tandem can be demanding: it requires specific techniques, chiefly teamwork and understanding between the two riders. The front rider, or captain, is responsible for communicating approaching changes in road surface, upcoming corners and gear changes. The rear rider, or stoker, must listen to instructions coming from the captain and minimize any unpredictable movements or changes in weight that can unbalance the bicycle.

The mechanism used to transfer power to the wheels from two sets of pedals can vary considerably. The commonest system is a synchronized chain drive where the two sets of pedals are linked and work together to power the rear wheel. More complicated systems have independent drive chains that allow one rider to stop pedalling and relax while the other carries on.

Right: Netherlands Men's Tandem cyclists Jan Mulder and Jeron Straathof in action during the Men's Tandem Cycling at the Sydney 2000 Paralympic Games held at the Dunc Gray Velodrome in Sydney, Australia.

Below: The Independent Drive system, developed by daVinci Designs, is unique to tandems and allows the captain and stoker to pedal or coast independently of one another.

THE CARGO BIKE

Bicycles are not just useful for transporting people but also for moving cargo. Before the widespread introduction of motorized vehicles, cargo bicycles were fundamental in the transportation of freight, equipment and other goods. They have been made in every size and shape imaginable and put to use everywhere – from factory floors to market stalls, and from small family businesses to large companies.

Soon after the creation of the modern bicycle, cargo bicycles began to be used by tradesmen to speed up deliveries. Often described as butcher's bikes or baker's bikes, they were used by all manner of tradespeople including postmen, milkmen and street traders. Designs varied but would usually include some form of wooden or steel box mounted over one of the wheels, where extra weight could best be supported.

Another common type of cargo bicycle is the porteur. First used by newspaper couriers in Paris, porteur bicycles feature a rack above the front wheel that is supported by the front fork or axle. While their cargo capacity is relatively small, just enough for a few bundles of newspapers, they are flexible and easy to produce.

Although still popular across the world, cargo bicycles are perhaps most conspicuous in the Netherlands – where they are known as *bakfietsen* ('box-bikes') – and Denmark. Still commonly used and manufactured today, the *bakfiets* typically consists of a frame with a longer wheelbase and a large cargo container positioned either between the wheels or over the front wheel.

A delivery boy makes use of a cargo bike, delivering goods for a business based in Shoe Lane in the City of London, c.1925.

SCHWINN CRUISER

c.1930

During the first decade of the nineteenth century the United States experienced what is often referred to as the 'first bicycle boom'. This was sparked by a series of vital design innovations such as the safety bicycle and pneumatic tyres and accelerated by modern assembly lines and methods of mass manufacture. Over the following few years Chicago became the centre of a golden age of bicycle manufacturing that saw the US producing more than a million bicycles a year, with a reported third of all patents registered at this time related to bicycle design and manufacture. However, as the motorcar and motorcycle came to prominence, the boom proved short-lived and many bicycle manufacturers closed down.

Arnold, Schwinn & Company was founded during this period in Chicago by the German émigré Ignaz Schwinn (1860–1945), and was one of the few manufacturers that survived the decline through diversifying, and identifying new markets. During the 1930s the company started producing a new bicycle that was marketed to children. The AeroCycle was based on the design of contemporary motorcycles and featured oversized balloon tyres, an imitation fuel tank and a chromed headlight. The bicycle was an immediate success and over the next few years the AeroCycle evolved into what became known as the 'American cruiser' or 'paperboy bike'. The cruiser's expressive styling, upright ride position and wide tyres were a perfect fit for the new suburbs in post-war America. Continued sales meant it was America's most popular bicycle until the late 1950s, establishing Schwinn as the dominant bicycle manufacturer throughout the twentieth century.

An illustration taken from an advertisement for the Schwinn AeroCycle model 34 in 1934. Designs such as the AeroCycle spawned a new style of bicycle, dubbed the 'American cruiser'. The designs were quickly copied by other manufacturers and cruiser-style bicycles were soon popular throughout the US.

THE AEROCYCLE

MODEL 34

■ ■ THE OUTSTANDING DESIGN IN 1934 ■ ■ ■

FRAME —
16 or 18 inch with truss fork — motorcycle design — welded one piece.

TIRES —
26 x 2⅛ inch Cord Balloon.

TANK —
Streamlined, with the top tube and head covered, and the trim lines of the latest motorcycle designs.

Has ample room for tool and other storage and clips for holding 1 or 2 standard No. 6 dry batteries. All wire outlets are rubber insulated.

The new headlight with its beautiful winged chromium bezel is built into the front of the tank.

SADDLE —
Padded bucket type.

HANDLEBARS —
Chromium braced, with large rubber grips.

PEDALS —
High grade, rubber.

GUARDS —
Wider and deeper, the streamlined automobile type with aluminum finish.

RIMS —
Deep drop center, chromium finish.

COASTER BRAKE —
New Departure, Morrow or Musselman.

CHAIN GUARD —
Chromium plated — does away with any danger of accident to fingers or clothing in the sprockets or chain.

LUGGAGE CARRIER —
Welded steel, special design.

ELECTRICAL EQUIPMENT —
New headlight, special taillight and horn. All receive their current from the batteries in the saddle tank. Lights are controlled by a central switch located on top of the tank.

COLOR —
Red and aluminum, as illustrated.

ARNOLD, SCHWINN & COMPANY • CHICAGO

RALEIGH ENGLISH ROADSTER WITH STURMEY-ARCHER AW 3-SPEED HUB

1930–40

The Raleigh Bicycle Company is one of cycling's oldest and best-known brands. It was founded in 1887 after businessman Frank Bowden (1848–1921) bought a new bicycle having received advice from his doctor to exercise more. Bowden was so impressed by his purchase that he returned to the small bicycle workshop, in Raleigh Street, Nottingham, England, bought the business and began to expand. In little more than seven years the company had moved to a new, 3-hectare (7-acre) site and become the largest bicycle manufacturer in the world.

Of all the models manufactured by Raleigh, the classic English Roadsters of the 1930s have left the greatest legacy. Featuring a new type of gearing system, the bicycles sold more than a million units and are still popular in Asia, Africa and parts of Europe. Built by Sturmey-Archer, another Nottingham company acquired by Bowden, the rear-wheel internal-gear hub allowed the cyclist to select a gear using a lever mounted to the handlebar. The Sturmey-Archer AW 3-speed hub was the most successful of these systems. While the hub was a complicated piece of engineering comprised of tiny components, it performed well with a long and largely maintenance-free lifespan. Still in production today, the Sturmey-Archer hub became one of the cornerstones of Raleigh's success.

Two posters from the 1930s vaunt the innovations of the Sturmey-Archer bicycle. Here was a bike, it seems, that could be ridden even by the unhealthy!

THE GOOD FAIRY OF ALL GOOD CYCLISTS

STURMEY ARCHER

HUB GEARS AND HUB BRAKES

THE GEARS THAT MAKE CYCLING EASY
BRAKES THAT MAKE CYCLING SAFE

BSA AIRBORNE PARATROOPER BIKE

The practicality, flexibility and durability of the modern safety bicycles soon saw them operated by the military for a variety of applications. Initially used to replace horses, which were expensive, resource-heavy and, on occasion, temperamental, bicycles were utilized in reconnaissance, messaging, first aid and cargo transportation. The use of bicycles spread and by the end of World War I all factions had made use of bicycle-mounted cavalry divisions.

The Birmingham Small Arms Company's Paratrooper bike was manufactured specifically for use by the British Army in World War II. Equipped with its own parachute, it was dropped from planes to provide easy, quick and unobtrusive transport for soldiers to move through enemy territory. To help the descent the bicycle was designed with a simple folding mechanism and a compactable seat tube and handlebars that ensured that there was no damage to the frame upon landing. BSA produced more than 60,000 units of the Paratrooper design and they were used extensively throughout the war, including many historic events such as the D-Day landings.

Modern warfare has little need for bicycles, and while the military continues to use them, their capacity is much reduced.

Right: A Paratrooper from the 1st Airborne Division, photographed with the BSA bike in 1942.

Below: While the BSA Paratrooper is perhaps the most recognizable bicycle ever used in combat, most armed forces of most countries have relied on bicycles at some point in history. While Sweden and Switzerland had particularly notable bicycle divisions, the Vietcong and North Vietnam forces used bicycles to great effect during the Vietnam War.

VÉLOSOLEX

While the term 'moped' – a portmanteau of 'motor' and 'pedal' – is now used to describe any form of low-powered vehicle, it originally referred to vehicles that combined low-powered motorcycle engines with bicycle pedals.

The earliest incarnations were either standard bicycles that had been retrofitted with small motors to assist pedalling, or early motorcycles that were fitted with chain drives and pedals to help when starting from a stationary position. Eventually a new object type evolved and the moped was born.

With more than 8 million units sold until production was stopped in the late 1980s, the VéloSoleX is the most popular incarnation of the moped. It was initially conceived during World War II when the French carburettor manufacturer Solex fitted a 45cc engine to the front wheel of a standard bicycle, transmitting power via a ceramic roller touching the wheel. The success of the VéloSoleX was immediate, with the relatively cheap manufacturing costs and low fuel consumption proving attractive during a difficult period in post-war Europe. Various models were produced for more than 40 years in France; in addition, licensed versions were produced in Eastern Europe and China.

In 2005 the Italian automotive design company Pininfarina redesigned the original VéloSoleX machine. While based on similar principles to the old machines, the new range of VéloSoleX mopeds rely on electric rather than petrol motors.

Advertisement by René Ravo for VeloSoleX, c. 1950. In 1947 Solex commissioned BP to develop a type of fuel marketed toward VeloSoleX users. Sold in cans under the name Solexine, it was a mixture of 6 per cent oil per litre of petrol and was specifically designed for use with mopeds.

VELOSOLEX

GARANTIE
1an

René
Ravo

FLYING PIGEON PA-02

The Flying Pigeon is synonymous with cycling in China. Since the first Flying Pigeon was produced in 1950 more than 500 million units have been made, making it not just the most popular bicycle ever produced, but the most popular *vehicle* ever.

In 1949 the Flying Pigeon Bicycle Company was officially sanctioned by Chairman Mao as New China's first bicycle manufacturer. Revolutionary China was a regimented society, with labour, agriculture, political beliefs and cultural values tightly controlled and legislated by the central Communist state. The bicycle was the approved form of transport and the Flying Pigeon quickly became emblematic of the regime, to the point that in the 1970s China's reformist leader Deng Xiaoping defined prosperity as 'a Flying Pigeon in every household'.

The bicycle remains a popular form of transport in China, and while Flying Pigeon sales have dwindled in recent years, largely owing to the increasing popularity of electric bicycles, the machine's longevity and sturdy construction have ensured that it is still one of the most common vehicles in China.

Cyclists negotiate the busy, polluted streets of Beijing. Recently China and the Far East have seen a dramatic rise in sales of electric bicycles. In a country with urban areas as densely populated as China, the bicycle, electric or not, remains one of the most efficient forms of transport available.

PARIS GALIBIER

c.1947
Harry Rensch

The Galibier is a lightweight racing machine that takes its name from a mountain pass hidden in the French Alps near Grenoble that is frequently used during the Tour de France. Designed by Harry Rensch, it was manufactured by his East London–based workshop, PARIS Cycles.

The Galibier's unique frame comprises a pair of narrow parallel top tubes combined with larger-dimension down tubes and an offset seat tube. This unusual geometry is specifically designed to resist transverse forces and help maximize the efficiency of the cyclist, making the most of every ounce of effort. This is achieved by eliminating what is known as 'frame whip', a flexing of the frame caused by excessive force exerted on the pedals when a rider ascends a hill or when sprinting. Any deformation of the frame can absorb the rider's energy, causing a considerable loss of efficiency. Conversely, the frame allows a certain elasticity, thereby helping to dampen any shocks received to the wheels and noticeably improving the handling of the bicycle at racing speeds.

The Galibier has a small but enthusiastic following and a new, updated version is now produced to order by the London company Condor Cycles.

Details of a modern PARIS Galibier hand-built by Condor Cycles, showing the narrow twin top tubes and the highly detailed lugged steel frame construction.

GRAN SPORT DERAILLEUR

1949
Gentullio Campagnolo

Until professional racing began to adopt derailleurs in the late 1930s the majority of cyclists used either single- or two-speed machines. The two-speed machines featured rear wheels with different-sized sprockets on each side hub. To change gears, the rider needed to stop, remove the wheel, flip it over, re-tension the chain and tighten everything up again. In the days when stages of the Tour de France could be as long as 480 kilometres (300 miles), this was not only impractical but extremely laborious.

It is said that, in 1924, a keen amateur cyclist named Gentullio ('Tullio') Campagnolo (1901–83) was racing through the snow-covered Dolomite Mountains when his cold hands were unable to undo the frozen nut on the rear wheel. Unable to change gear, Campagnolo lost the race and thereupon resolved to redesign the entire system. After first developing a rod-based quick-release system, Campagnolo set up his own manufacturing company and released the Gran Sport in 1949. The Gran Sport was the first example of what has become known as a 'parallelogram derailleur', and, while not a huge commercial success, it set the blueprint that every modern derailleur has followed.

Founded in 1933 in the Vicenza workshop of Tullio Campagnolo, the company soon developed into an industry leader and provided componentry for most of the top cyclists, including Tullio Campagnolo's good friend Eddy Merckx. Campagnolo still produce high-end groupsets, near-complete collections of a bicycle's mechanical components, used by many professional cyclists.

M1 'F-FRAME' MOULTON BICYCLE

1962
Alex Moulton

The Moulton Bicycle Company was the brainchild of the respected British engineer and inventor Dr Alexander Moulton (1920–2012), a specialist in rubber, who was responsible for developing the revolutionary rubber suspension system on the Mini.

Inspired by the dwindling public confidence in the supply of oil in the wake of the 1956 Suez Crisis, Alex Moulton – along with many others – reassessed alternatives to oil-based transport. Convinced that human-powered solutions were a suitable alternative, he set about designing a new bicycle. First released in 1962, the M1 'F-frame' Moulton was a small-wheeled bicycle featuring a small rubber suspension system. Chiming perfectly with the prevailing mood of the 'swinging sixties', the bicycle created quite a stir, and its immediate success caused other manufacturers, such as Raleigh, to quickly bring out their own small-wheeled machines.

The commercial success of the design was matched by its performance, inspiring a loyal following of small-wheel bicycle enthusiasts that has continued to grow. In this sense, the Moulton acted as a type of 'disruptive technology' for the bicycle industry, forcing it to re-evaluate a machine whose fabrication and design had been fixed for so long. The supporters of small-wheeled bicycles point out that such designs are invariably lighter with better acceleration, cause less aerodynamic drag and produce a riding sensation and handling that, they claim, has more of a 'feel' to it.

Along with the Mini and the Mary Quant mini-dress, the F-frame Moulton became an emblem for fashion and the cultural scene that flourished in London in the 1960s. However, the design's ride quality and sheer technical virtuosity ensured that its influence spread much further than that of any stylistic fad.

RALEIGH CHOPPER

1969
Ogle Design &
Alan Oakley

Inspired by the American youth craze for high-rider bikes and the chopper motorcycles made popular by films such as *Easy Rider* (1969), the Raleigh Chopper has become something of a cultural icon to people from a certain generation. Rather than producing just another smaller-scale version of an adult's bicycle, the Chopper was styled from top to bottom specifically with the youth market in mind. The result was something new and cool with which children identified.

The first prototype was based on a combination of an early concept design by the British firm Ogle Design, and a sketch that the head of Raleigh's design department, Alan Oakley (1927–2012), made on the back of an envelope during a flight home from the United States. The bicycle featured 'ape-hanger' handlebars, a rear wheel larger than the front, and a spongy motorcycle-style saddle that incorporated a backrest.

Throughout the 1970s and into the '80s the Raleigh Chopper was incredibly desirable, with the bicycles loved by those who owned them and coveted by those who did not. Raleigh had been in a state of decline before the release of the Chopper, but by the end of the 1970s the Chopper had sold more than 1.5 million units in the UK alone.

A child reclines on a Chopper's motorcycle-style backrest on the streets of Liverpool, UK. Although the bike was hugely popular for more than a decade, its eye-catching design was not without problems. Chief among these was the difficult handling caused by shifting the centre of gravity further back than on a standard bicycle.

DAWES GALAXY 1971

Bicycle touring is a long-distance cycling discipline, often taking place over a number of days and embarked upon for pleasure as much as for competition. It can involve a day spent leisurely travelling between two rural locations, a two-week holiday across Europe, or a weekend charity ride.

A touring bicycle is a specialist machine that must be robust enough to withstand lengthy rides without maintenance, be comfortable enough for the rider to tolerate consecutive days in the saddle, and be capable of carrying heavy loads. Touring bicycles usually feature an extended wheelbase (the distance measured between the wheels), in order to avoid the risk of the pedals getting caught up in the luggage and pannier racks.

When the British cycling manufacturer Dawes launched the Galaxy in 1971, it set a new benchmark for accessible touring bicycles. Prior to this, tourers were typically expensive custom-built cycles, but the Galaxy was a commercially available off-the-peg machine that helped make touring a realistic prospect for the casual cyclist.

The Galaxy range is still in production today and remains popular more than 40 years after it was first introduced.

EDDY MERCKX'S HOUR RECORD BICYCLE

1972
Ernesto Colnago

One of the most enduring records in any sport, the hour record, represents the longest distance cycled in a single hour. With no team tactics, no terrain and no weather, it is the ultimate test of a cyclist's ability. While the first official record was made in 1893 by the founder of the Tour de France, Henri Desgrange (1865–1940), many consider the Belgian cyclist Eddy Merckx (1945–) as the cyclist who laid down the first modern hour record.

Often credited as the greatest all-round cyclist in the history of the sport, Merckx won the Tour de France five times, the Giro d'Italia five times, and the Vuelta a España once, as well as being a four-time winner of the World Championships. He undertook the record in Mexico City, covering 49.431 kilometres (30 miles) at high altitude. Even for a rider of Merckx's stature, breaking the hour record was a particularly gruelling experience, after which he claimed it was 'the hardest ride I have ever done'.

During the 1990s the hour record started to change hands with increasing frequency. Concerned that the hi-tech bikes and resultant riding positions were making it difficult to compare the skill, strength and stamina of the cyclist, the Union Cycliste Internationale (UCI) – cycling's governing body – decided to ban 'unconventional' equipment, and in 2000 all records dating back to 1972 were reclassified.

Although used as benchmark for any bicycle undertaking the hour record attempt – a blueprint to which all attempts at the record must now conform – Merckx's bicycle was anything but standard. Designed by the Italian frame builder Ernesto Colnago, the bicycle had a super-lightweight frame, a titanium stem requiring specialist welding in Detroit, and holes drilled extensively through the handlebars and chain. These factors helped reduce the total weight to a little over 5.5 kilograms (12lb).

Eddy Merckx at the starting line of the Agustín Melgar Velodrome in Mexico City about to start his attempt at the hour record, 1972. The choice of venue was due to the high altitude, which ensures air that is less dense than at sea level, reducing the drag forces acting on the rider.

OLE RITTER
48.653,92 KMS.
EDDY MERCKX
49.406,88 KMS.
NUEVO RECORD.

BIKE SHARING SYSTEMS – VELOS JAUNES

Bicycle-sharing systems are increasing in popularity, with every self-respecting modern city either already operating one, or in the process of developing one. When successfully managed and carefully designed, a bicycle sharing scheme can have a significant impact on the mobilization of a large metropolis.

The first sharing schemes were organized by local community groups, often in a very ad hoc and spontaneous manner. These usually involved providing a fleet of bicycles to be used in an unregulated fashion and left for the next user. Perhaps unsurprisingly, few of these schemes were hugely successful, with the bicycles quickly ending up either stolen or vandalized. The exception to this was the Vélos Jaunes ('Yellow Bikes') scheme, initiated by the French city of La Rochelle in 1975. Widely regarded as the first genuinely successful scheme, a modified programme, Yélo, is still in use in the city today.

The majority of today's successful schemes, however, are based on Lyon's 2005 Velo'v programme using 'Smart Bikes'. Such systems are usually government-operated, often in association with a corporate partner, and use electronic locks, smart cards, telecommunication systems and on-board computers.

Schemes such as Paris's Vélib' and London's Barclays Cycle Hire use aggressive pricing structures that often make brief short-distance trips free but extended day-long hire expensive. This encourages the constant replenishment and movement of units throughout the network.

Bicycles from Paris's Vélib' initiative. The scheme was launched on 15 July 2007 with bicycles and 750 automated rental stations. The network has since doubled in size and is the largest system of its kind in the world.

BREEZER SERIES I

In the early 1970s a group of young cycling enthusiasts, many of whom were keen amateur and semi-professional road cyclists, started to spend their evenings and weekends racing down the Mount Tamalpais trails in northern California. Not many people can claim credit for helping to create an entirely new discipline of cycling, but this group of friends and acquaintances had sown the seeds of a bicycling subculture that would have an impact they could hardly have imagined.

Initially starting out using pre-war balloon-tyre Schwinn cruisers, the riders soon started to modify their machines with better brakes, tyres and strengthened frames. These heavily adapted bicycles, referred to by the riders as 'klunkers', continued to develop and gears were soon added to help the riders reach new rides farther up the mountain trails. Eventually, the limitations of using modified bicycles became too great and it became necessary to build bespoke machines. In 1978 Joe Breeze (1953–) built a prototype of the Breezer Series I – the first purpose-built mountain bike.

As the popularity of the discipline increased, regular races were held. These started to attract riders from further afield and by the mid-1980s the sport of mountain biking was fully established across both the United States and Europe.

Right: Framebuilder and mountain bike pioneer Joe Breeze (on the right) with his blue Breezer #1, and Charlie Kelly with the nickel-plated Breezer #2.

Below: Early mountain bikers using an adapted bicycle. These modified American cruiser-style bikes were referred to as 'klunkers'.

AVATAR 2000

1980
David Wilson,
Richard Forrestall &
Harald Maciejewski

A recumbent bicycle is one that places the rider in a reclined, laid-back cycling position. Much like the standard bicycle, recumbents come with a wide range of frames and components available. This includes configurations with long and short wheelbases, different-sized wheels, over-seat and under-seat steering, rear- or front-wheel drive, and with full, partial or no suspension.

Other than the obvious visual disparities, recumbents offer notable performance differences to standard upright bicycles. The most significant of these is the aerodynamic advantage provided by the smaller and lower profile, which essentially improves their straight-line speed. Many designs reduce the aerodynamic drag even further by installing full or partial coverings called 'fairings'.

However, recumbents are not without their disadvantages. Issues such as reduced manoeuvrability, difficulties with steep gradients, lower visibility – both of the road and of the bicycle itself – have prevented the recumbent from achieving the popularity of its more accessible, and flexible, relation.

While custom-built recumbents have been around since the birth of the bicycle, it wasn't until the Avatar 2000 was released in the late 1970s that they became commercially available. Designed by the UK-born professor of engineering David Wilson (1928–) and bike shop owners Richard Forrestall and Harald Maciejewski, the influential long wheelbase design is usually credited with starting the modern recumbent bicycle movement. Successful throughout the 1980s, the Avatar 2000's popularity reached a peak when the actor Christopher Walken rode one in the science-fiction film *Brainstorm* (1983).

A more relaxed, comfortable form of cycling? Many cyclists adopt recumbents to alleviate the neck and back pain associated with uprights. Recumbents known as handcycles also enable those with little or no use of their legs to engage in cycling.

KLEIN BICYCLES

c.1980
Gary Klein

Gary Klein built his first bicycle in 1972 when he was a student studying chemical engineering at the Massachusetts Institute of Technology (MIT). Its pioneering design was one of the first uses of an oversized aluminium frame. After graduating, he set up Klein Bicycles to commercialize the process, specializing in racing and road bikes before later moving into mountain bikes.

Klein's new aluminium frames offered numerous advantages over other frames typically built from steel or its variant alloys such as chromoly (CRMO). Chief among these was a better strength-to-weight ratio, effectively meaning that an aluminium bike will be lighter than a steel bike of equivalent strength.

One of the initial barriers to aluminium construction was difficulties encountered when joining the frame tubes together. Until TIG (tungsten inert gas) welding became economically viable in the 1970s, potential stresses and fatigue in the joints were hard to avoid. The other downside to aluminium is that it does not have the strength of steel. In order to compensate for this, and gain extra strength, Gary Klein made his aluminium frames from oversized tubes. Another consequence of oversized tubing is a stiffening of the frame that helps minimize any losses in the power generated by a rider. While contemporary mountain bikes are made from a variety of different materials, many still use the oversize tubing system pioneered by Gary Klein.

Gary Klein continued to manufacture mountain bikes and road bikes, including this Attitude model from 1992. The success of the Klein designs and the innovative manufacturing techniques resulted in the company being bought by Trek in 1995.

BROMPTON

early 1980s
Andrew Ritchie

Viewed by many as the archetypal folding bicycle, the Brompton has been an enormous success. As with so many designs, it was born of a desire to improve upon a previous machine – the Bickerton folding bicycle. After evaluating the Bickerton, the UK engineer Andrew Ritchie (1947–) thought he could do better, and began to develop a new type of folding bicycle. The first few prototypes were built in Ritchie's bedroom. While they were rough and crude, the majority of the key design features – such as the pivoting rear triangle that allows the rear wheel to fold underneath – were already evident. After a few further refinements Ritchie started to produce the Brompton himself in small quantities. After a number of years, manufacturing the Brompton on a relatively small scale and barely turning a profit, a dedicated Brompton factory was finally established in Brentford, London, where the bicycles are still made today.

The unique folding mechanism and high-class ride quality have established Brompton as the ideal choice for commuters and urban cyclists who need a bicycle that packs away small enough to stow on public transport, can be easily carried up staircases, and hidden away under tables or in the cupboards of small flats. The Brompton achieves all this with an effortless grace that inspires fierce loyalty from the large number of happy owners, many of whom have owned their machines for many years, updating and replacing components as they become worn or outdated.

Owing to the Brompton's elegantly resolved mechanism, the bike can be folded up in seconds. For many owners this means that the bicycle is a constant presence in their daily lives, used on the commute to work, folded away and stored in the corner of their office during the day, and then stowed under a table in their living room during the evening.

SPECIALIZED STUMPJUMPER

1981
Tom Ritchey &
Specialized

At the start of the 1980s mountain biking was still in its infancy, with the majority of bicycles being made in relatively small numbers by specialist frame builders. The Stumpjumper was the first mass-manufactured mountain bike and one of the major factors in the huge rise in popularity that saw sales of mountain bikes overtake those of road bicycles by the end of the 1980s.

The Stumpjumper was based on a bicycle custom-built by Tom Ritchey (1956–), one of the original mountain-bike frame builders. Specialized Bicycle Components, a major US bicycle brand, took this design and devised a way of creating a similar machine using mass manufacturing and standardized components. After extensive research, suitable components were internationally sourced from locations including Italy, Switzerland and France, and shipped to Japan for assembly.

The result of this new approach to mountain bike production meant that Specialized were able to sell the Stumpjumper at less than half the cost of the cheapest custom-built alternative. While a number of the traditional bicycle retailers were initially sceptical of this new discipline of cycling, it soon became apparent that consumers didn't share their reservations. The initial shipment of Stumpjumpers sold out in a matter of weeks and a new craze in cycling was born.

The Specialized Stumpjumper first went on sale in 1981. Priced at around $850, it cost significantly less than the hand-built mountain bike, which at the time was the only other option.

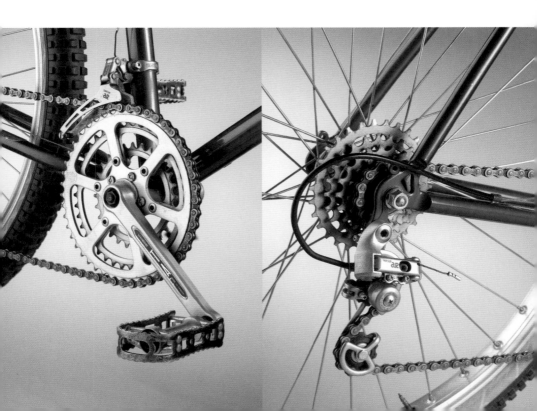

KUWAHARA *E.T.* MODEL BMX   1982

BMX, or bicycle motocross, began in the 1970s when, inspired by the popular motocross stars of the day, a group of friends started to organize dirt-track bicycle races in California. While they started out using standard wheelie bikes, such as Schwinn Stingrays and Raleigh Choppers, these were soon customized for better performance. By the end of the decade the sport had captured the imagination of children all over the United States, and purpose-built tracks and bikes soon followed.

As well as dirt-track racing, other BMX disciplines began to emerge, the most famous of which is freestyle. Often described as BMX stunt riding, freestyle was pioneered by Bob Haro (1957–) in the mid-1970s when he and his friends began riding their bicycles through the concrete reservoir channels in San Diego, California. Gaining in popularity, freestyling soon spread to skateparks and on to the city streets. Riders like Bob Haro became well-known stars, performing tricks at public demonstrations and competitions, and designing their own bikes.

Although already popular in the States, and to a lesser extent in Europe, BMX received a huge boost in 1982 when film director Steven Spielberg spotted children BMXing in the streets and asked Bob Haro to perform the stunts in *E.T.* The worldwide success of *E.T.* helped popularize BMX and was responsible for inspiring an entire generation of children.

The appearance of BMX bikes in *E.T.* played a major role in encouraging children to take up the sport. Many of today's most famous cyclists, such as Sir Chris Hoy, the most successful Olympic cyclist of all time, first took up the sport after watching *E.T.*

"ET" #3003

AM SERIES MOULTON BICYCLE 1983

Alex Moulton

A few years after the enormous success of the original 'F-frame' (see page 40), Moulton Bicycles was acquired by Raleigh. Freed from the restrictions of overseeing day-to-day construction, Alex Moulton was once again able to devote more time to research and development. Along with various automotive projects he continued to refine his designs for small-wheeled bicycles, and in 1977 he first conceived the spaceframe. The brief for this new model was straightforward – to combine the responsive, small-wheel ride quality and ethos of the original Moulton with modern engineering to produce a hi-tech, lightweight performance bicycle.

As the collaboration with Raleigh had now ended, Alex Moulton bought back the rights to the name, re-equipped the original factory to manufacture the new spaceframe design, and launched the first models in 1983. The unusual-looking frame was constructed using a complex configuration of thin steel rods that were carefully engineered and placed to produce the required rigidity while remaining exceptionally lightweight. Both the initial models featured full suspension systems, with the rear suspension based on the principles of rubber compression that Moulton developed for earlier models.

In addition to its striking appearance, the Moulton spaceframe was an exceptional performer, helping cement its place among the most popular touring bicycles ever made. The series is still in production today and is continually updated with new models.

The key to the AM Series Moulton bicycle's excellent performance is the stiffness generated by the space-frame geometry. This ensures that very little of the rider's energy is lost through unnecessary flexing of the frame. The exceptional stiffness also improves the handling, providing secure road holding and sound cornering.

FRANCESCO MOSER'S HOUR RECORD BICYCLE

1984
Moser Cycles

In 1984 Francesco Moser (1951–) became the first cyclist to break Eddy Merckx's long-standing hour record, and to achieve a distance of over 50 kilometres (31 miles). He did so using a new style of bicycle that was among the first to prize aerodynamic principles as highly as lightweight components.

In the early 1980s wind-tunnel testing proved that solid disc wheels provided a significant improvement in aerodynamic performance. Moser – a strong believer in using technology to drive performance – took advantage of this and, although not yet ratified as legal equipment by the UCI, he fitted disc wheels to an unusual new frame design.

Disc wheels slice through the air much more efficiently, reducing the drag caused by traditional spoked wheels by around half. They make handling much more difficult, especially in high crosswinds when too much steering torque is often generated, but for short races and for indoor velodromes the performance benefit was clear.

The raised seat position accommodated a rear wheel with a larger diameter than the front. The design of the bike proved extremely influential and went on to revolutionize mainstream road racing in the years that followed.

Francesco Moser made a number of attempts at the record, often using experimental bicycles. One unsuccessful attempt featured a bicycle whose rear wheel had a diameter almost twice that of the front.

In his quest for the hour record, Francesco Moser had a total of 15 different bicycles built. This is the one that was ridden during his successful 1984 attempt.

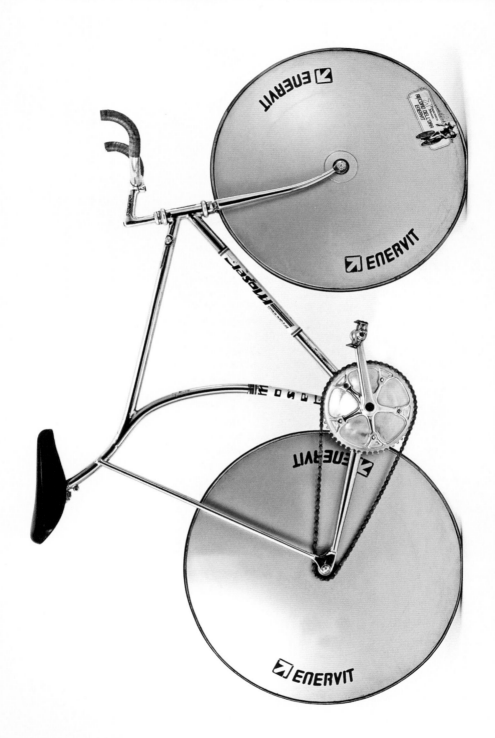

CINELLI LASER

1983
Gilberto Colombo

The Cinelli Laser was one of the most expensive bicycles ever developed, and the first in the new breed of so-called 'aero bikes'. This marked an entirely new way of designing bicycles developed from the bottom up, based around a modern understanding of aerodynamic principles and new hi-tech testing methods.

Built by the Italian engineer Gilberto Colombo (1921–88), one of the Laser's most radical departures from traditional construction were the unusual frame tubes, which in cross section had a droplet-shaped profile. In order to maximize the effect of any aerodynamic advantage, the complicated profile needed to be precise and consistent. The tubes had no lugs that could cause drag at the joins, but were instead attached with linings of sheet metal that were sanded down at the seams. Such exacting requirements necessitated a high degree of skill and craftsmanship in the manufacturing of the frames.

Another innovative design feature – now taken for granted in racing bicycles – was the reconfiguration of all the components to ensure that they were either streamlined for maximum aerodynamic efficiency, or shielded in the slipstream of other components. The most obvious example of this was the Laser's miniaturization of the steering components, which dramatically reduced a crucial part of the bicycle's front profile.

After the first production models were used in the 1983 Pan-American Games, Cinelli developed numerous commercial and professional versions for both road and track.

Top: The Rivoluzione Pista was an unusual-looking variation of the Laser from 1985. It included a specially strengthened frame in order to facilitate the removal of the seat tube.

Bottom: Aleksandr Kirechenko of the Soviet Union rode a Cinelli Laser during the 1km time trial at the 1988 Seoul Olympics. Kirechenko won the gold medal despite getting a flat tyre on the penultimate lap.

SLINGSHOT MOUNTAIN BIKE

1985
Mark Groendal

As with many innovations, there was a degree of coincidence and luck involved in the creation of the Slingshot frame. Its designer, Mark Groendal, came up with the concept when he noticed that the mini-motorbike he was riding had suddenly become more comfortable. After a closer look he found that the bottom tube had fractured, allowing the front end of the motorcycle to flex more and better absorb any impacts.

A few years later Groendal began to experiment with these ideas and built a prototype BMX that completely omitted the traditional down tube, replacing it with two steel cables attached to the bottom bracket with springs. While this BMX was a crude prototype that even used a cut-up ski to provide a flexible top tube, the principles behind it proved to be sound. As well as acting as a form of suspension, helping to smooth away any bumps and lumps in the track, the sprung cable also helped return energy usually lost during the pedal stroke, thus improving the efficiency of the energy transfer. After further development Groendal established a company with his brother, before releasing the first Slingshot mountain bike in 1985.

The Slingshot immediately captured the attention of the mountain biking community, shocking both riders and frame builders with a design that appeared to flaunt conventional thinking and seemingly defy the laws of physics.

The engineering principles used in the original slingshot design have been developed further and Slingshot models are now available for BMX, Cyclo-Cross and road racing as well as mountain biking. A number of other manufacturers, including Biomega, have also used similar principles to produce bicycles with wires instead of down tubes.

STRiDA

1985
Mark Sanders

While studying industrial design engineering at London's Royal College of Art, Mark Sanders was undertaking a daily 22-mile commute into central London. Fed up with trying to squeeze his bicycle on to a train, Sanders decided to design a new folding bicycle, and thus the STRiDA was born. It is based on the shape that offers the simplest geometry, but which is also the strongest – a triangle. The frame quickly folds up into what the designer refers to as a 'stick-with-wheels', which can then be easily wheeled around, stowed neatly in corners or even packed in a golf bag to take on a plane.

The STRiDA is not designed for extended journeys but is intended for people who cycle no more than 6 kilometres (3.7 miles) a day. Aimed solely at the city commuter market, it needs minimal maintenance. The Kevlar belt that replaces the chain and the internally routed cables, hidden within the frame, make the bicycle oil free.

The STRiDA divides opinion. Some people love its simplicity, the oil-fee chain and the sheer idiosyncrasy of the design. Others are unable to feel comfortable with the feather-light handling, the extra-small wheels and the short wheelbase. Regardless of how people feel about the STRiDA, it is noteworthy for defying people's expectations of how a bike should look and perform.

Top right: This isometric engineering drawing shows the complexity and the number of components that went into creating what seems a straightforward machine.

Bottom right: The strong geometric shapes of the STRiDA make it an eye-catching design.

Below: The STRiDA is perfect for negotiating London's Underground and rail network.

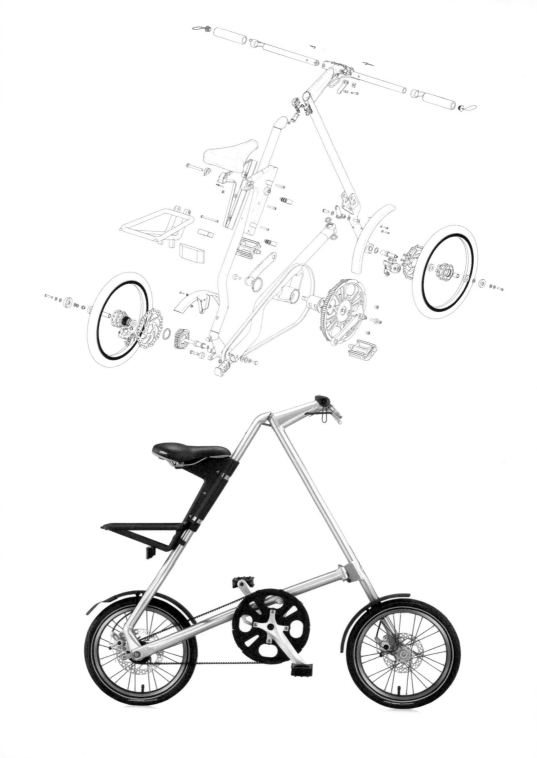

BATTAGLIN PIRANA

Featuring the first carbon-fibre monocoque shell frame exclusively designed for road race use, the Pirana was well ahead of the curve. However, as carbon fibre manufacturing was still in its infancy, the process was hugely expensive. The process was also still relatively crude and resulted in a frame that was actually slightly heavier than the metal alternatives. Unlike the machines that followed, carbon fibre was chosen not to save weight, but because it was the most suitable material to create a frame with the necessary geometry to place the rider in the required aerodynamic position. According to the bicycle's manufacturer, Giovanni Battaglin, this position resembled an egg with the small end pushed forward.

In addition to its innovative frame, the bicycle's other unusual feature is the front disc wheel. Shaped like a bubble, it required a specially widened and strengthened front fork. This was designed to act as a form of fairing, which shields and hides the non-aerodynamic forms of the feet, cranks and pedals.

The Pirana, built specifically to be used by Roberto Visentini, the leader of the Carrera racing team, was regrettably never raced. When unveiled at the starting line of the 1985 Giro d'Italia prologue, it looked so markedly different from any of the other machines, and caused such a stir, that – although at the time there were no specific rules regarding bicycle design – the race jury refused to allow the Pirana's participation in the race.

The Battaglin Pirana is one of the most unusual and striking Italian race bikes ever created. The bubble disc wheel was designed to reduce drag.

MONTY TRIALS BIKE

c.1985
Pere Pi

Trials riding – sometimes referred to as observed trials – is a competitive discipline of mountain biking inspired by motorcycle trials. Participants are required to negotiate complicated courses filled with natural or man-made obstacles without allowing any part of their body to touch the ground. The courses are an extreme test of the rider's skill and require tremendous balance and precision handling.

While the original trials bicycles were hybrid designs that combined elements of mountain bikes and BMXs, a specialized typology quickly emerged. Trials bicycles rely on extremely wide wheels with rims to provide extra traction and aid balance. They are single-geared machines, with a ratio chosen to provide the power and quick acceleration needed at the typically low speeds of trials riding. Since competition riding does not require a seat, the bicycles are often designed without one.

The sport originated in Catalonia, Spain. Pere Pi, a nine-time Spanish Motorcycling Trials champion, wanted a bicycle for his six-year-old son Ot to practise trialling. Pere converted a standard bicycle by removing all the large components, such as the guards and lights, before fitting wide handlebars and tyres. As Ot practised, it became clear the sport of trials would be possible on a bicycle as well as on a motorcycle.

As bicycle trial-riding events started to appear in tandem with motorcycle events, a new scene developed, and Pere founded Monty Bicycles to manufacture bespoke designs. Ot Pi went on to win multiple World Championships in trials events, riding Monty bicycles designed by his father.

Many trials bikes do not have a seat, because competitive riders are always out of the saddle. A bicycle with one of its most recognizable features removed can look a little unsettling, making us re-evaluate the machine's function.

KESTREL 4000

Carbon fibre and carbon-fibre composites are the most prevalent materials used in the manufacture of high-end sport equipment. They provide super-lightweight structures that offer unparalleled strength and rigidity. However, until US bicycle manufacturer Kestrel released their pioneering design, the only carbon fibre found in bicycles was limited to some smaller components, or the occasional prototype monocoque frame. During the late 1980s Kestrel produced a series of innovations that made them one of cycling's biggest names, and began the trend toward the type of carbon-fibre manufacturing that still defines the construction of today's performance machines.

The Kestrel 4000 was the first carbon-fibre bicycle in the world. The carbon-fibre technology used in the bike emerged from the Californian aerospace industry.

Released in 1986, the Kestrel 4000 was the first all-carbon production bicycle. It was also the first bicycle frame to be designed using finite element analysis (FEA), a technique used to analyse the forces exerted at different points across a structure. This procedure is commonplace today, but it was revolutionary at the time and helped the designers understand more about the stresses and strains at work in a bicycle frame.

Although the Kestrel 4000 was a commercially available production bicycle, the costs involved in early carbon fibre manufacturing were prohibitive. This meant that, other than professional riders, only the wealthy could afford them, helping cement the machine's reputation in the US as a 'dentists' bike'.

BOTTECCHIA TT BIKE
WITH SCOTT AERO BARS

On the eve of the final time-trial stage of the 1989 Tour de France, Laurent Fignon held a seemingly insurmountable 50-second lead over his nearest rival Greg LeMond. Fignon, a very capable time triallist, was expected to ease to victory. However, over the 25-kilometre stage LeMond gained more than two seconds per kilometre over Fignon and secured his first Tour de France title in the process.

By and large the machines used by the riders were identical. The only difference between LeMond's steel-framed Bottecchia bicycle and the others was the crucial addition of aero bars. Designed by Boone Lennon, a former alpine skiing coach, aero bars were an innovative new technology pioneered in triathlon cycling. As renowned aerodynamics expert Steve Hed commented: 'Here was something that didn't cost a lot and you could just put it on your bike and go faster.'

The benefits of aero bars are twofold. Most importantly, the resulting head-down, arms-stretched-out position is super-streamlined, minimizing the rider's profile. Wind tunnel tests have shown that 80 per cent of a cyclist's energy simply goes into pushing air out of the way, and any reduction in the front profile can have huge benefits. The other benefit is the manner in which the rider's forearms sit on the aero bars, distributing the upper body weight evenly throughout the skeleton, allowing a sustained period of riding in an optimum power output position. While it is possible to achieve a similar position using traditional drop handlebars, the resulting muscle tension absorbs, and therefore wastes, energy. Aero bars have been measured to save up to three minutes in a 40-kilometre time trial.

American cyclist Greg LeMond seen riding down Avenue des Champs-Élysées in Paris, France on his way to victory in the 1989 Tour de France. Although aero bars are now considered essential time-trialling equipment, the bars seen on LeMond's bike were thought revolutionary at the time.

LOTUS TYPE 108

1992
Lotus & Mike Burrows

If a single bicycle could illustrate the impact of new materials, manufacturing and design, the Lotus Type 108 would be it. The project began when engineer and cycling enthusiast Mike Burrows took his new bicycle to Lotus Engineering for testing. The Lotus team put this prototype in the wind tunnels usually used to develop racing cars. Surprised by the results, they agreed to put their own expertise into further improving it. British cyclist Chris Boardman then became involved and agreed to ride the machine in the 4,000-metre pursuit at the 1992 Barcelona Olympics.

When Boardman arrived in Barcelona with the Type 108, people were astonished. Its sleek shape and black carbon-fibre monocoque design resembled something from science fiction, and the majority of the 60 million viewers had never seen anything like it. Breaking the world record twice in the early rounds, Boardman achieved something even more remarkable in the final. In pursuit cycling, two competitors start the race simultaneously at opposite sides of the track, with the winner being the cyclist who posts the fastest time. Alternatively, one rider can chase the other down, thus winning the race. This is almost unheard of, especially in an Olympic final, but it is exactly what Boardman did, overtaking his rival on the final lap and claiming the gold medal.

The Lotus 108 was quickly dubbed the 'Superbike' by the press and public. Lotus went on to create a time-trial version of the bicycle, the Type 110, which Boardman would later ride in stages of the Tour de France, and for a successful attempt at the hour record in 1996.

Chris Boardman rounding the bend of the Barcelona velodrome as he rides to gold in the 1992 Olympics. The introduction of the Lotus 108 led to what has been described as an 'arms race' in cycling, where design and technology were continually improved to the point where the authorities took steps to limit what was termed 'technological doping'.

'OLD FAITHFUL'

1993
Graeme Obree

Graeme Obree (1965–), or the 'Flying Scotsman' as he is often called, is one of cycling's true iconoclasts. He operated outside the world of professional cycling, largely without any help from sponsors or bicycle manufacturers, or support from cycling teams or governing bodies.

In 1993 Obree surprised the cycling world when he broke Francesco Moser's world hour record (see page 64), using a bicycle he designed and built himself from a variety of scavenged components, including parts from an old washing machine. The bicycle, named 'Old Faithful', was unlike anything else used at the time. Notable innovations included a new crouched riding position, with the hands tucked in under the rider's chest, and a narrow bottom bracket that brought the rider's legs very close together.

Obree's initial attempt at the record fell short by almost a kilometre, but as the track was booked for a full 24 hours he returned the next morning for a second attempt. This remarkable feat of stamina and mental strength paid off and Obree was successful in the second attempt.

Obree's record stood for just one week before it was broken by the English cyclist Chris Boardman (1968–), prompting Obree to return to his workshop and develop a new riding position. Dubbed the 'Superman position', it required the rider's hands to be held in an extended position directly in front of the head. Over the next few years Boardman and Obree traded the hour record and success at the World Championships back and forth in what became British cycling's most celebrated rivalry.

Graeme Obree riding 'Old Faithful', the bicycle he designed and built himself. The idiosyncratic riding position was referred to as the 'crouch position' and produced a particularly efficient and aerodynamic shape.

MIGUEL INDURAIN'S PINARELLO ESPADA

1994
Pinarello

Meaning 'sword' in Spanish, the Espada was designed and built with input from an aerodynamics engineer who worked in Formula One. The results of the collaboration utilized technology that, at that time, was more commonplace in high-performance motorsport. The carbon-fibre monocoque frame acted as an external skin, supporting the loads and stresses directly without the need for internal loadbearing tubes. Monocoque shells can provide greater stiffness and less weight than a traditional diamond-shaped bicycle frame.

The Espada was built specifically for the Spanish professional cyclist Miguel Indurain (1964–) and first used on the track when he broke Graeme Obree's hour record in 1994. Three other versions were subsequently produced, with later models complete with gears and internal cables hidden within the monocoque frame for use on the road.

While the Espada was an innovative bicycle that pushed the limits of technology, it was not the only reason behind Indurain's success, with the Spanish cyclist's unique physique also giving him a distinct advantage. Known to most people as 'Big Mig', Indurain was a time-trial specialist and five-time winner of the Tour de France (1991–5). His size might have been expected to be a disadvantage, due to the extra height and weight that he carried compared to other cyclists. However, his unique physiology allowed his blood to carry a phenomenal amount of oxygen around his body – about twice as much as an average adult. He also had a vast lung capacity and a resting pulse as low as 28 beats per minute. All of this gave him an advantage over not just the average person, but also professional cyclists.

Miguel Indurain broke the hour record using the Pinarello Espada at the Vélodrome du Lac in Bordeaux, France, 1994. He also used the Espada in two victorious time-trial stages during his final Tour de France victory in 1995.

TREK Y-FRAME

By the start of the 1990s US bicycle manufacturer Trek felt they had taken frame building as far as possible using traditional chromoly and aluminium construction. In order to develop the performance of their products, they started searching for new lightweight alternatives. After a meeting at an aerospace industry trade show, a Trek engineer was introduced to a carbon-fibre moulding company called Radius. This fundamentally shifted the focus of the company's designs toward this new material. After a few years of refinement, Trek introduced a new carbon-fibre construction method, called OCLV (Optimum Compaction, Low Void), which optimized the compression of the carbon fibres within a thermoset epoxy base, resulting in the lightest mountain bike frame ever made.

Continually pushing its technology, Trek combined OCLV construction with the monocoque skin designs that had been successfully introduced in high-performance track and time-trial machines. First released in 1995, these Y-frame designs were full-suspension mountain bikes unlike anything seen before.

Although some complained about the performance and durability of the early Y-frame models, Trek's inventive use of carbon fibre influenced the design of mountain bikes for years to come.

The Y-33 was one of Trek's original Y-frame designs. The frame geometry and manufacturing techniques proved popular and have been widely used and adapted for use by other manufacturers in other disciplines of cycling.

AIRNIMAL CHAMELEON

Not just a great daily bike for commuting or popping to the shops, with a few minor adjustments the Chameleon is entirely capable of competing in elite road races. The Chameleon is regularly used by professional athletes, once even being ridden to a bronze medal in a Triathlon World Championships.

The British company Airnimal spent four years developing the Chameleon, with many components requiring specialist design and manufacture. The frame is predominately aluminium, with a carbon-fibre fork, and an elastomer-based rear suspension system. The frame sits on unusually sized 24-inch (61cm) wheels, which fall somewhere between the size of those on an orthodox racing bike and those used on small-wheeled racing machines.

On top of this, the Chameleon is a folding bicycle, with four different states of folding. As well as the unfolded, ride-ready state, there is a semi-compact stage where the rear fork folds away under the frame enabling the machine to fit easily into a car boot. This can be achieved in seconds without any tools. A more complex degree of folding can be achieved with some basic tools and a few extra minutes, enabling the bicycle to fit into a travel suitcase. Finally, 15 minutes, and an even more detailed procedure, sees the bicycle packed away into a rucksack.

The Chameleon's extremely flexible design is easy to take on an aeroplane, and provides excellent performance, along with good all-round comfort. All this makes it the perfect choice for an international touring bike.

BIOMEGA MN-01

2001
Marc Newson

Biomega was among the first in a new wave of manufacturers that attempted to redefine the way that bicycles are perceived and valued. Sometimes referred to as 'designer bikes', these machines are created to be a lifestyle choice as well as a functional solution.

The Danish company was founded with the aim of making bicycles to suit the new urban landscape of contemporary cities. Working with design luminaries such as Marc Newson, Ross Lovegrove and Karim Rashid, the goal was to create bicycles that challenged people's preconceptions of traditional bicycle building and enabled the rider to reconnect with the city environment.

Such a strong and unapologetic focus on appearance could easily lead to style over substance. However, Biomega's clever design and manufacturing solutions ensure that function and performance are very much at the forefront of the development process. This is demonstrated by enclosed and sealed gearing and drive-chain systems that put an end to grease-stained clothing, along with construction technologies taken from aerospace industries.

Biomega's first model, the MN-01, was created by Australian designer Marc Newson (1963–) and set the blueprint for the company's philosophy. The striking zigzag frame brings to mind a bent steel girder but is actually made from a material described as superplastic aluminium. This was a first for bicycle manufacturing and required the frame to be constructed from two separate shells glued together using a process of epoxy bonding previously used solely in the construction of jet engines.

Marc Newson's MN range comes in a variety of models with differing specifications. The MN-01 Extravaganza is the flagship model and has won accolades from the worlds of industrial design, engineering and the bicycle industry.

BIANCHI PISTA CHROME

Fixed-wheel, single-speed bicycles are far from a modern idea. It is the same mechanism that was utilized by the velocipedes of the mid nineteenth century (see page 10). After the invention of the freewheel hub, fixed wheels were typically used only on track bikes and the occasional road-race bike. However, the past couple of decades have seen an emergence of a cycling subculture focused on fixed-wheel bicycles. 'Fixies', as they are commonly referred to, were pioneered by bicycle couriers, before gaining traction with a larger community of urban cyclists.

The rear sprocket of a fixie is attached directly to the wheel hub, forcing the cyclist to continue pedalling whenever the bicycle is in motion. This fixed mechanism is also used to control the speed of the machine, with a higher cadence, or rate of pedalling, resulting in higher speeds. Conversely, by resisting the forces of the pedals, the speed can be reduced.

This is an entirely different style of cycling, whose supporters claim gives a better sensation of connection to the bicycle. However, fixies are not best suited for the casual cyclist. They require constant concentration and an awareness of what your legs are doing at all times. This technique tends to attract serious cyclists, who are extremely passionate about their bicycles, often modifying and customizing their machines to suit their individual preferences.

The urban fixed gear market is increasingly important for most bicycle manufacturers. Bianchi's 2012 range includes five different versions of urban fixed-gear Pista, three of which are shown here.

YIKEBIKE

2010

The YikeBike was created by a team of engineers and entrepreneurs from New Zealand with the intention of dramatically changing urban transport. Providing city dwellers with a fast, safe and easy way to navigate their environment, the YikeBike is one of the smallest and lightest electric folding bikes in the world. Its carbon-fibre construction means it can be carried on trains and buses, lifted up stairs and stored under a desk or in a cupboard. The battery provides a range of 10 kilometres (6.2 miles) from a charge of 30 minutes.

As significant as these details are, it is the YikeBike's dynamic reinterpretation of the orthodox riding position that really sets it apart from other electric bikes. The shape of the YikeBike has been described as a 'mini-farthing' design, with the handlebars unusually positioned behind the rider just below the seat. This unique, and initially disconcerting ride position, has prompted much debate. Some users enjoy its openness and the greater visibility it affords; others cannot get used to the absence of a handlebar to the front of them, which would give the arms something to brace against when decelerating or braking.

The YikeBike's unorthodox appearance is the machine's most unique and marketable feature, but also the reason people are often initially cautious. In order to ensure the rider's safety, YikeBikes has anti-lock brakes and are restricted to a top speed of 23kph (14mph).

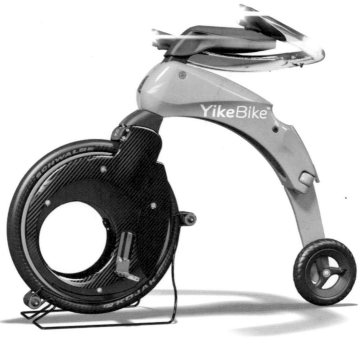

VANMOOF NO.5

The Vanmoof is a no-nonsense bicycle in which simplicity is key. Manufactured in the Netherlands, it is inspired by classic Dutch city bikes such as the *omafiets* (see page 20). Responding to the fact that more than half the world's population now live in an urban environment, Vanmoofs are specifically designed with the modern city and the urban commuter in mind. This includes stripping the bicycle of all non-essential items and the inclusion of a lightweight, rust-free frame.

The oversized aluminium frame is the main reason for the bicycle's distinctive look. However, there is nothing decorative about the frame, which, along with the rest of the Vanmoof's components, is purely functional. The oversized tubes give the rigidity needed for practical use, as well as providing enough space to house some of the design's more inventive features. Along with the necessary brake cables and other wires, the frame stores a built-in heavy-duty lock. This can be pulled from a slot in the top of frame and then retracted when not in use. The unusual top tube also projects out past the front fork, and behind the seat tube, which gives the extra space needed to encase a front and rear light.

The Vanmoof reduces the bike to its simple outlines, almost like a child's drawing. Sturdy and resilient, it is perfect for the urban environment, whether it's the cobbled streets of Amsterdam or the hectic roads of London.

PINARELLO TEAM SKY DOGMA 2 2011

In 2012 Bradley Wiggins (1980–) became the first British rider to win cycling's most prestigious race, the Tour de France. In addition to the years of hard work, bespoke training regimes, specialist diets and large support teams, the cutting-edge equipment used by Team Sky played a large part in the historic victory.

A single stage of the race can be as long as 250 kilometres (155.3 miles). In order to stand up to these prolonged pressures, a successful racing bicycle needs to be comfortable, durable and suitable for a variety of different terrains and road surfaces. According to the UCI regulations, to be eligible for the Tour de France the design must be constructed using a main triangle shape, and must also be commercially available.

Along with the rest of the Team Sky squad, Wiggins rode a modified Pinarello Dogma 2. One of the world's most advanced road bicycles, the Dogma 2 features an unusual asymmetric frame. This was devised as a response to the fact that, with the chain, gears and other drive transmission elements all located on the right-hand side of the frame, bicycles are not symmetrical. Using computer modelling software such as Finite Element Analysis (FEA) and Computational Fluid Dynamics (CFD), along with physical laboratory testing, the Pinarello designers studied the forces acting on each side of the frame, and layered the carbon fibre accordingly. This produced a frame that is stronger and stiffer on the side where forces are at their greatest.

Right: Bradley Wiggins riding round the Arc de Triomphe during the twentieth and final stage of the 2012 Tour de France. His Dogma 2 has the yellow livery that signifies the leader of the Tour.

Below: Detail of the Dogma 2 frame.

EADS AIRBIKE

2011
Bristol Aerospace
Innovation Centre

The Airbike is the first fully functioning bicycle to be constructed using a process called 3D printing – an automated method of generating three-dimensional objects directly from computer models. 3D printing, or additive manufacturing as it is sometimes known, creates objects by splitting them into a series of tiny layers. Each of these thin layers is then 'printed', with the object taking shape as successive layers are built up on top of each other.

In the case of the Airbike, components were slowly built up by fusing together thin layers of nylon powder, each just one-tenth of a millimetre thick. Even complicated components like the bottom bracket were printed as a single element, complete with bearings and other moving parts. Although this technology is not yet perfected, the benefits are already apparent. In the future, individual components, or even whole bicycles, could easily be built to the buyer's own specifications at minimal extra cost. As the bicycles are constructed from a small number of preformed components, with large sections printed in single pieces, there is no conventional maintenance or assembly.

The Airbike is still very much a prototype and was created as a means of highlighting the potential of 3D printing. As such, the prototype is not a highly specified, high-performance machine, but more an indication of what is to come. Experts have predicted that production versions of 3D-printed bicycles will be available within the next decade.

Details of the computer-aided design and additive layer manufacturing process used to create the Airbike. This new type of digital fabrication has the potential to revolutionize not just bicycle manufacturing but many other industry manufacturing processes.

TEAM GB TRACK BIKE 2012

Over the past ten years, Great Britain has dominated the world of competitive cycling. Much of this has been due to the ongoing successes at key competitions such as the Olympic Games and World Championships. At the 2008 Beijing Olympics, Great Britain won 14 medals, including 8 golds. This level of dominance is difficult to sustain, but Britain again topped the medal table at the London 2012 Olympics with a further eight gold medals. To put this into perspective, no other country won more than a single gold cycling medal during the same games.

While the focus and the accolades quite rightly go to the athletes, the equipment used is fundamental to this success and can help give an all-important advantage. British Cycling's in-house design team, led by former cyclist Chris Boardman, has been developing its own bespoke equipment, in relative secrecy, since 2001. After the Beijing Olympics the technical regulations were changed, and any equipment now used must be commercially available, and pass inspection by cycling's governing bodies. In reality, this has not stopped British Cycling making their own equipment, but their equipment is now available for purchase – if you have enough money.

Every item of equipment used by the British team now carries a sticker to prove it has been ratified by the governing bodies and adheres to the rules. However, the team's continued success still leads, in some quarters, to disquiet about discrepancies in the equipment. This resulted in the playful accusations by the French team that the British cyclists must be using 'magic wheels'.

Great Britain's Chris Hoy celebrates after crossing the finish line, to win the gold medal in the London 2012 Olympic Games men's keirin final.

MANDO FOOTLOOSE

2012

Mark Sanders &
Han Goes

The electric bicycle is cycling's biggest growth market – especially in the Far East, where sales of e-bikes in places like China now outstrips those of cars and motorcycles. The Footloose is a new collaboration between the Korean automotive manufacturer Mando and the designer of the STRiDA, Mark Sanders (see page 70).

The bicycle features cutting-edge electric technology developed for the automotive industry, applied to bicycle design. Rather than the pedals directly driving the wheel, a chainless hybrid system is used. The mechanical energy from pedalling is converted to electrical energy via an alternator and is then fed directly to the battery. By pedalling, the rider can noticeably extend the standard 30-kilometre (18.6-mile) range.

The motor is controlled by a throttle on the handlebars. An array of sensors connected to a computer chip and central control unit constantly assess the speed, terrain and slope of the road in order to regulate the performance of the motor, and adjusts the gears using an intelligent automated system.

The battery, sensors and control unit are all hidden within the frame. A detachable LCD display panel is mounted on the handlebars keeping the rider informed of important information such as speed, distance cycled, remaining battery power, and amount of electricity being generated by the pedals. Finally, the bicycle has a simple folding mechanism allowing for easy storage and transportation.

When riding the Footloose, the act of pedalling provides an entirely different function to that of a direct drive system. The technology required to do this enables the rider to customize a number of the bike's features, such as acceleration, pedal resistance and gear ratios, using a software interface rather than a mechanical one.

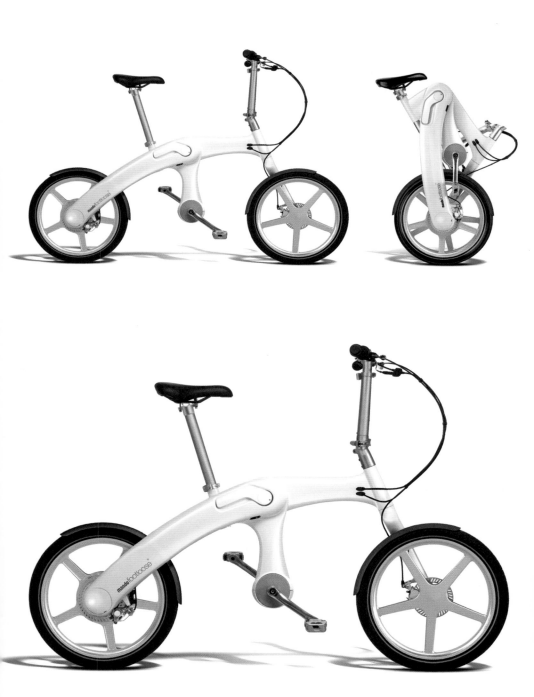

FARADAY PORTEUR

The team behind the Faraday Porteur set themselves the challenge of designing the ultimate utility bicycle for modern living. Originally created as a concept for a design competition, the bicycle was developed further and brought to the point of production using support provided through the funding platform Kickstarter. Along with similar crowd-funding platforms, Kickstarter draws on the support of a networked collection of individuals who pool their resources, via a managed website, to give financial backing to small-scale creative projects.

The Porteur is an elegant electric bicycle, or e-bike, whose assisted power comes via a simple thumb-operated switch. The built-in lithium battery provides a range of 25 kilometres (15 miles) from a single 45-minute charge. More than enough to meet the demands of the 20-kilometre (12-mile) average distance that we now travel to get to work each day. As the name would suggest, the Porteur features a luggage rack above the front wheel with enough room to stow everything needed for a day at work, or even a weekend of recreation.

The Faraday Porteur takes its name from the bicycles first used by Parisian delivery boys to distribute daily newspapers as they came fresh from the printing presses (see page 24).

INDEX

PICTURE CREDITS

The publisher would like to thank the following photographers, agencies and bike companies for their kind permission to reproduce the following photographs:

2 Wende Cragg/Rolling Dinosaur Archives; 7 David Ditzler/Cooper Technica Inc; 9 akg-images; 11 Illustrated London News Ltd/Mary Evans Picture Library; 13 Mary Evans Picture Library; 15 Science Museum/Science & Society Picture Library; 17 David Ditzler/Cooper Technica Inc; 19 Martin Schluter Fotografie/Pedersen Manufaktur Kalkhoff GbR; 20 Stuart Kelly/Alamy; 21 Koninklijke Gazelle N.V; 22 da Vinci Tandems; 23 Adam Pretty/All Sport/Getty Images; 25 H. F. Davis/Topical Press Agency/Getty Images; 27 Pacific Cycle/Schwinn; 28-29 Nottinghamshire Archives (DD/RN/4/23/1) & (DD/RN/4/23/2); 30 Bernhard Angerer/Embacher Collection; 31 Imperial War Museum; 33 Apic/Getty Images; 35 Forrest Anderson/Liaison/Getty Images; 36-37 Condor Cycles Ltd; 38 Campagnolo Srl; 39 Eric Norris; 41 Moulton Bicycle Company; 42 Image courtesy of The Advertising Archives; 43 Paul Trevor;

45 Dawes Cycles; 48 Eddie Linssen/Alamy; 50 Erik Koski; 51 Wende Cragg/Rolling Dinosaur Archives; 53 Richard Howard; 55 Bernhard Angerer/Embacher Collection; 56-57 Brompton Bicycle Ltd; 59 Specialized; 60 Kuwahara International Co. Ltd; 61 Universal/Kobal; 63 Moulton Bicycle Company; 64-65 J.P Praderes; 67 below Mike Powell/Getty Images; 67 above Gruppo Srl; 69 Slingshot Bicycle Company; 70-71 Ming-Cycles/MAS Design Products Ltd; 73 Battaglin Cicli Srl; 75 Monty; 77 Howard Yao/aberrance.com; 78 AFP/Getty Images; 79 John Pierce/Rex Features; 81 below SSPL/Getty Images; 81 above Graham Watson; 83 Matthew Polak/Sygma/Corbis; 85 Jacques Pavlovsky/Sygma/Corbis; 87 Trek Bikes; 90 David Perrin/Marc Newson; 91 below Lena Paaske/Marc Newson; 91 above Tue Schiorring/Marc Newson; 92-93 Bianchi; 94-95 YikeBike Ltd; 96-97 Vanmoof; 99 Doug Pensinger/Getty Images; 101 EADS UK Ltd; 103 Carl de Souza/AFP/Getty Images; 104-105 Meister Inc/MAS Design Products Ltd; 107 Faraday Bikes.

Every effort has been made to trace the copyright holders and we apologize in advance for any unintentional errors or omissions, and would be pleased to insert the appropriate credit in any subsequent publication.

CREDITS

An Hachette UK Company
www.hachette.co.uk

First published in Great
Britain in 2013 by
Conran Octopus Ltd
in association with
The Design Museum

Conran Octopus Ltd,
a division of Octopus
Publishing Group Ltd
Endeavour House
189 Shaftesbury Avenue
London WC2H 8JY
www.octopusbooks.co.uk
www.octopusbooksusa.com

Text copyright © Octopus
Publishing Group Ltd 2013
Design and layout
copyright © Octopus
Publishing Group Ltd 2013

Distributed in the US by
Hachette Book Group USA
237 Park Avenue
New York NY 10017 USA

Distributed in Canada by
Canadian Manda Group
165 Dufferin Street
Toronto, Ontario, Canada
M6K 3H6

All rights reserved. No part of
this work may be reproduced
or utilized in any form or by
any means, electronic or
mechanical, including
photocopying, recording or
by any information storage
and retrieval system, without
the prior written permission of
the publisher.

ISBN 978 1 84091 630 0

A CIP catalogue record for
this book is available from the
British Library

Printed and bound in China

10 9 8 7 6 5 4 3 2 1

Text written by:
Alex Newson

Publisher:
Alison Starling
Consultant Editor:
Deyan Sudjic
Editor:
Alex Stetter
Copy Editor:
Robert Anderson

Art Director:
Jonathan Christie
Design:
Untitled
Picture Research:
Anne-Marie Hoines

*Assistant Production
Manager:*
Caroline Alberti